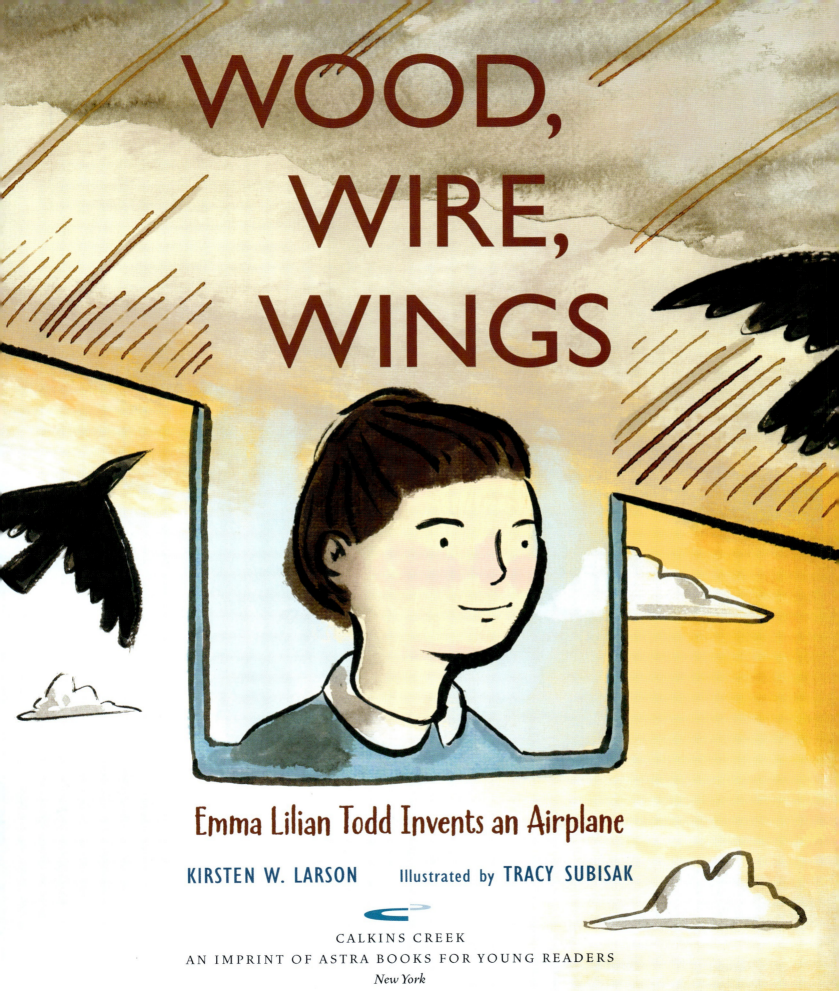

WOOD, WIRE, WINGS

Emma Lilian Todd Invents an Airplane

KIRSTEN W. LARSON   Illustrated by **TRACY SUBISAK**

CALKINS CREEK
AN IMPRINT OF ASTRA BOOKS FOR YOUNG READERS
New York

To **Emma Lilian Todd**, problems were like gusts of wind: they set her mind soaring.

Sometimes the problems seemed small, like where to find metal to craft her inventions. (Solution: she saved tin cans from her supper.)

But soon Lilian's challenges ballooned.

Lilian grew up in a time when it seemed like everyone
was tinkering . . .

1886
Josephine Garis Cochrane
patents the dishwasher
(early model on right).

1870s
Alexander Graham Bell
patents the telephone.

1850s
The first mass-produced watches
are developed by
American Watch Co. (early watch on right).

1868
Christopher Latham Sholes, Samuel Soulé, and Carlos Glidden
invent the typewriter (early model on left).

1901
Guglielmo Marconi sends the
first radio transmission across
the Atlantic.

1879
Incandescent light bulb is patented
by Thomas Edison
(early light bulb on right).

1851
Isaac Singer patents a practical sewing machine
with many more to follow
(early model on left).

1870
Pneumatic subway is
built by Alfred Ely Beach
in New York.

. . . including Lilian's grandfather, who invented his own carriage wheel. Just like Grandfather, Lilian whittled and fiddled, turning dreams into useful inventions.

One winter Lilian rescued a broken toy from the trash and snatched a ball off the Christmas tree. She trimmed and twisted, filed and fitted.

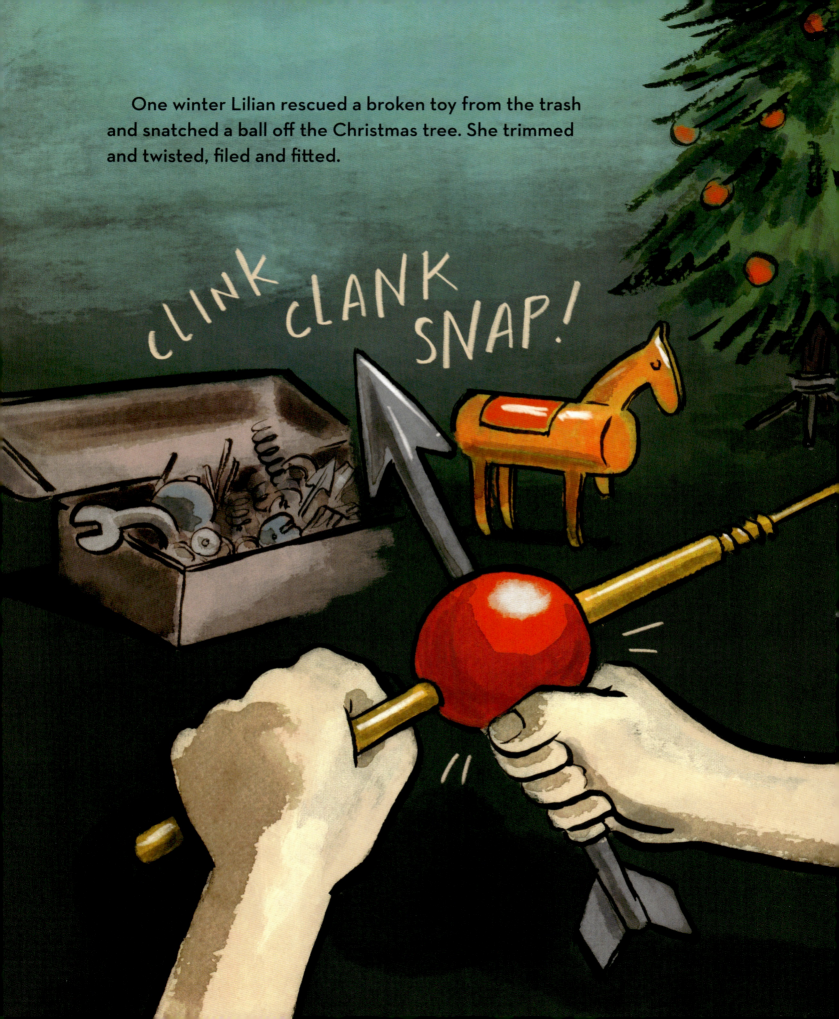

Would the weather vane work? Lilian took it outside for a test. When the wind blew, the weather vane pointed true. *Success!*

Another day she took apart a clock, spreading the pieces before her. Did this wheel fit here? Did that lever fit there? She put the pieces back this way. No tick.

She put the pieces back that way. No tock. The clock stayed still. *Failure!* Lilian stood baffled, yet buoyed by the challenge.

"Ever since I can remember I couldn't have a piece of tin or wire in my hands without bending it and twisting it to make something. . . . I was always making things, and my mother saw to it that I wasn't discouraged, that I had the tools I wanted."
—Lilian Todd, 1910

Lilian couldn't imagine a life without tools or tin, wires or wheels. Yet inventing wasn't women's work, so she did the next best thing—she got a job typing up plans for new machines at the U.S. Patent Office. While Lilian's fingers raced across the keys, she constructed each contraption in her mind.

Soon blueprints for fantastical flying machines flooded the office. But could they really fly? Lillian *needed* to know.

thwp!

Lilian fixed her eyes on a new horizon—a future of flight. She tinkered with tiny aircraft in her new Manhattan apartment after long days of typing—winding rubber-band propellers to send small airships soaring. Stitching balloons, which bobbed and bounced from the ceiling.

While Lilian tinkered and tested, other inventors flew the first full-sized airplanes. But when she read the news, she simply shook her head. Their designs still seemed fantastical—not practical.

Lilian vowed to build something better—an airplane with sloping wings to glide like a bird and a cockpit for two.

"The machine of
the Wright brothers has to be
navigated by its operator lying
flat . . . and waving his legs
in the air. My machine will be
operated by a woman, I hope, and she
will swing in a basket below and balance
it . . . as automatically as does a
person riding a bicycle."
—Lilian Todd, 1908

Lilian spent hours considering the crows circling overhead, studying the angle of an albatross's wing, and constructing models that hung like chandeliers from the ceiling.

Before long, her airplane took over her apartment—then it took over her life.

Amidst the parts and pieces, Lilian's bird emerged from bamboo covered in canvas.

At last she strapped a doll into the basket and sent it soaring. It dipped, then dove . . . straight down!

Crash! The airplane and its passenger smashed to pieces. With a second model, Lilian's hopes took flight once more . . . But her model didn't.

Failure! Lilian stood there baffled, but buoyed by the challenge. Then on the third try her model slipped into the sky. Until . . .

Whap! A slight mishap when a wire snapped. Yet it was a breakthrough. Now Lilian knew: an airplane built from her design could fly.

SNIP
CLINK
SNAP

"The men make fun of the way
I construct my models . . . but they
admit that my ideas are all right and
that a full sized aeroplane built in
accordance with those same despised
models will fly—which is the principal
thing after all, isn't it?"
—Lilian Todd, 1908

By 1908 Lilian realized her ballooning project couldn't cram into her apartment. She was simply short on space . . . and short on money too. What could Lilian do to keep her dream aloft? Why, tackle each setback one by one, like a pilot ticking off a checklist.

Get money. *Check.* (She asked Olivia Sage, one of the richest women in the world.)

"I have always been interested in [Lilian] because I think she is a capable woman and I like to see women do things."
—Olivia Sage, 1910

Find space. *Check.* (She hired the Wittemann Brothers to assemble the airplane at their plant.)

Sketch a frame of sturdy spruce. *Check.*

Buy supplies—muslin, army duck, and piano wire to put it all together. *Check. Check. Double check.*

A year later, there was one box left to tick: find an engine.

At that time suitable airplane engines were hard to come by—as scarce as women working with wood and wire. Instead, Lilian had to make do with a car engine.

At last, her plane was ready for takeoff.

An airplane crafted by a woman was quite a curiosity. So, no surprise, Lilian chose to showcase her plane at the 1909 Interborough Fair in New York, where it captivated crowds alongside cannons catapulting ladies through the sky.

As the fair-goers crushed close, Lilian readied her plane for liftoff.

But the engine sputtered.

The plane shuddered.

It wouldn't budge at all.

Failure!

Buoyed by the challenge, Lilian brainstormed her next steps.
Secure space to work throughout the winter. *Check.*
Study motors and revise her design. *Check.*
Score another engine. An *airplane* engine. *Double check.*

Since the engine company crafted just two a month, Lilian knew she would have to wait, and wait, and wait some more. For almost a year, while tweaking and tinkering with her design.

When the engine finally arrived in the fall of 1910, Lilian checked the final box: install the engine.

She gave it a whirl. The new engine purred. The propeller whirred.

Lilian's dreams were ready to soar once more.

"It's a work that grips you.
I work myself seventeen hours
a day often, and then fuss because
I've got to go to bed and waste
time sleeping."
—Lilian Todd, 1910

On November 7, 1910, cars lined a road along a field and crowds crushed close to watch the latest marvels—daring pilots demonstrating flying machines. Some were fantastical. Others, like Lilian's, were quite practical.

As the day dragged on, slicing, icy winds whipped across the plain. One pilot scuttled his flight, declaring it too windy to fly. Lilian worried about the weather. Should she wait and waste her chance?

Lilian wouldn't wing it. She had waited four years to see her plane lift off. She could wait a few moments more.

When the winds died down, Lilian made her final checks and found the best spot to study her airplane's every dip and dive.

At last Lilian's pilot drove the plane onto the field, bouncing across the grass, picking up speed.

Faster. Faster. Faster.

Until . . . *success!*

It lifted off, soaring toward the future . . .

BBRRRMM BRRMMMM

"Will I guide it myself? Well,
I think perhaps during the experimental
stages I may simply observe its actions,
but later on I surely will drive it."

—Lilian Todd, 1910

. . . filled with flying.

"There is no work so discouraging,
so exasperating, so delightful, so mean,
so difficult, so exhilarating
as building aeroplanes. . . ."
—Lilian Todd, 1910

Author's Note

Lilian Todd works in her New York City studio, around 1908. This studio also served as a meeting place for the Junior Aero Club, which Lilian founded that same year.

The Wright brothers invented the airplane in 1903. When I was growing up, their success seemed like the end of the story. But what I've learned from a lifetime of living and working around planes is that the Wright Flyer was just a beginning. Being the first to make something doesn't always mean your solution is the best one. Engineers spend as much time improving existing designs as creating new ones.

The Wright brothers' airplane was an amazing achievement. But imagine if pilots today still lay on their stomachs and slid their hips back and forth to help control the plane like the Wrights did! Inventors like Lilian Todd wanted to build planes that flew better and could be controlled like a car or bicycle. Every designer had his or her own ideas, and for many years each airplane built in the United States was unique. No two looked just alike. Each flight proved new ideas right or wrong and helped create the airplanes we know today.

While many early airplane designers competed to fly faster, higher, and farther, Lilian focused on making airplanes a practical form of transportation, like the trolley. Along the way she got her own patent for an invention to hold up papers while she typed. She also became the Aeronautic Society's first woman member and founded the Junior Aero Club in America, which taught children the science of flight and encouraged invention. After her airplane's successful flight, Lilian donated it to the New York National Guard, making the Guard the first state military to have an airplane.

Many of Lilian Todd's ideas don't survive in modern airplanes. She talked often of her planes' birdlike wings, yet airplanes today don't have them. Once tested, they might not have made the airplane fly any better. Yet other choices she made do survive, like the use of ailerons. These hinged surfaces, invented by Glenn Curtiss, were an improvement over the Wright brothers' idea of twisting the wings to control the airplane.

At places like the National Aeronautics and Space Administration (NASA), where I worked for six years, engineers still grapple with issues from Lilian's day, like making better engines and improving control during flight. They experiment with solar-powered and electric planes. They invent new designs for flying faster without making noisy sonic booms. And they create ways to automatically control airplanes to make them safer to fly.

There is at least one big difference from Lilian's day, though. Today many airplane engineers are women. I think Lilian would have liked that.

Top: Aeronautic Society member Lilian Todd displays her model during the Morris Park Air Meet, November 1908.
Bottom: Lilian Todd sits behind the controls of her plane in Richmond (now Staten Island), New York, September 1909.

The Age of Airships

Henri Giffard's dirigible

September 24, 1852—Henri Giffard of France flies the dirigible, a motorized balloon.

1891–1896—Otto Lilienthal of Germany makes more than two thousand glider flights in five years, showing that birdlike flight was possible.

May 6, 1896—Professor Samuel Pierpont Langley's Aerodrome No. 5 is the first large, airplane-like model driven by an engine to fly successfully.

The first flight of the Wright brothers, Kitty Hawk, North Carolina

December 17, 1903—America's Wilbur and Orville Wright make the first controlled, powered flight in an airplane; the Wright Flyer travels about 120 feet in 12 seconds. The Wright brothers work mostly in secret to keep their ideas from being copied.

1904—The World's Fair in St. Louis includes a special aeronautics display and prizes; the Wright brothers do not participate, but others graze the clouds in gliders, kites, and dirigibles. **Lilian Todd** works as a secretary at the fair, and her window overlooks the airfield.

October 23, 1906—Alberto Santos-Dumont of Brazil flies about 200 feet (60 meters) in France. **Lilian Todd** sees a picture of Santos-Dumont's design and believes she can devise a better one.

November 13, 1907—Paul Cornu of France makes the first-ever helicopter flight lasting 20 seconds.

June 1908—The Aeronautic Society of New York is founded to encourage experiments and share ideas; **Lilian Todd** becomes the only woman member.

Louis Blériot's monoplane

July 25, 1909—Louis Blériot of France flies 25 miles across the English Channel from France to England in his monoplane.

August 1909—America's Glenn Curtiss sets a new speed record flying 47 miles per hour in his Reims Racer.

November 7, 1910—Didier Masson takes **Lilian Todd**'s airplane for its first test flight. She becomes the first woman to design a successful airplane on her own.

Mr. Lincoln Beachey in Thomas Scott Baldwin's airship at the St. Louis Exposition, 1904

Selected Bibliography

Asterisks (*) in the following list indicate the sources of the quotations.

Primary Sources

"Aerial Craft in Warfare." *The Sun* (New York), Feb. 10, 1909. Chronicling America: Historic American Newspapers. Library of Congress.

Aeronautical Society of America. *Aeronautics*, vols. 5–7. Google Books.

"Aeroplane for Guardsmen." *The Sun* (New York), Jan. 26, 1912. Mrs. Russell Sage Collection. Auburn University Libraries.

"Another Attempt to Solve Aerial Navigation Problem." *The New York Times*, Jan. 7, 1906.

"Her Biplane a Success." *Brooklyn Daily Eagle* (Brooklyn, NY), Nov. 8, 1910. Old Fulton New York Post Cards.

"Hudson Celebration On." *The Sun* (New York), Sept. 5, 1909. Chronicling America: Historic American Newspapers. Library of Congress.

"Miss Todd Does Not Fly." *The Sun* (New York), Sept. 7, 1909. Chronicling America: Historic American Newspapers. Library of Congress.

"Miss Todd Has an Airship." *The Sun* (New York), Nov. 1, 1908. Chronicling America: Historic American Newspapers. Library of Congress.

"Miss Todd May Fly To-Day." *The Sun* (New York), Sept. 6, 1909. Chronicling America: Historic American Newspapers. Library of Congress.

"Miss Todd to Try to Fly." *The Sun* (New York), Sept. 13, 1910. Old Fulton New York Post Cards.

* "Mrs. Russell Sage at Flying Field." *The Sun* (New York), July 28, 1910, Old Fulton New York Post Cards.

"The Second Annual Exhibition of the Aero Club of America." *Scientific American*, vol. 95, no. 24 (Dec. 1906), pp. 447–49.

* "She Builds Aeroplanes: Protege of Mrs. Sage the Only Woman in the World Who Constructs Airships." *New-York Tribune*, Nov. 20, 1910, Chronicling America: Historic American Newspapers. Library of Congress.

State of California, Department of Public Health, Vital Statistics. Death Certificate of E. Lilian Todd. Pasadena, 1937.

"Teaching Boys Ballooning." *The Sun* (New York), March 1, 1908. Chronicling America: Historic American Newspapers. Library of Congress.

* Todd, Lilian. "How I Built My Aeroplane." *Woman's Home Companion*. Nov. 1909.

* "Woman Aviator Builds Aeroplane of Own to Race for Big Prizes." *Syracuse Daily Journal: The Journal's Daily Magazine*, June 20, 1910. Old Fulton New York Post Cards.

* "Woman Builder of Airship." *The Sun* (New York), Feb. 5, 1908. Chronicling America: Historic American Newspapers. Library of Congress.

"Woman Builds Airship; Birdlike Machine Soars." *Indianapolis Star*, Nov. 19, 1910.

* "Woman Inventor and Her Airship, Which Is Built on Lines of Crow." *The Evening World* (New York), Feb. 5, 1908. Chronicling America: Historic American Newspapers. Library of Congress.

* "Woman's Work." *Kingston Gleaner* (Kingston, Jamaica), 18 Nov. 1910.

"Woman Will Fly in New Aeroplane." *Geneva Daily Times* (Geneva, NY), Sept. 16, 1909. Old Fulton New York Post Cards.

"Women Want to Fly." *The Sun* (New York), Aug. 1, 1909. Chronicling America: Historic American Newspapers. Library of Congress.

"Young Woman Builds Airplane to Fly an Hour for U.S. Prize." *The Times-Dispatch.* (Richmond, VA), Feb. 7, 1908. Chronicling America: Historic American Newspapers. Library of Congress.

Books and Articles

Crocker, Ruth. *Mrs. Russell Sage: Women's Activism and Philanthropy in Gilded Age and Progressive Era America.* Bloomington: Indiana University Press, 2006.

Crouch, Tom D. "The Aeronautic Society of New York and the Birth of American Aviation, 1908–1918." *New York History*, vol. 92, no. 4 (2011), pp. 269–89.

Crouch, Tom D. *The Bishop's Boys: A Life of Wilbur and Orville Wright.* New York: W. W. Norton, 1989.

Crouch, Tom D. *A Dream of Wings: Americans and the Airplane, 1875–1905.* New York: W. W. Norton, 2002.

Goldstone, Lawrence. *Birdmen: The Wright Brothers, Glenn Curtiss, and the Battle to Control the Skies.* New York: Ballantine, 2014.

Hughes, Thomas P. *American Genesis: A Century of Invention and Technological Enthusiasm, 1870–1970.* Chicago: University of Chicago Press, 2004. Google Books.

Websites

Cooper, Ralph S. "E. Lillian Todd." Earlyaviators.com, 2023, earlyaviators.com/etodd1.htm.

PBS. "Technology Timeline: 1752–1990." *American Experience.* pbs.org/wgbh/americanexperience/features/telephone-technology-timeline.

Short, Simine. Simine's U.S. Aviation Patent Database. invention.psychology.msstate.edu/PatentDatabase.html.

Websites active at time of publication

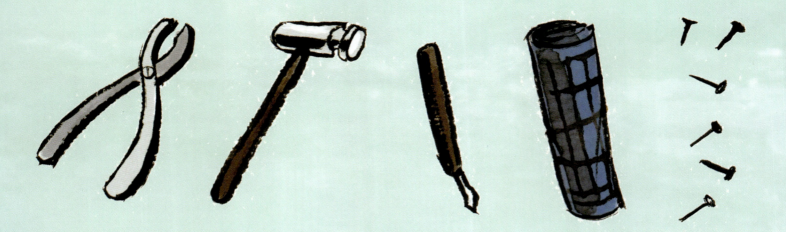

To Nils, Cooper, and Finley, with love and thanks —*KWL*
To Dad —*TS*

Acknowledgments

I would like to thank all those who helped this story take flight. Special thanks to Bill Rogers for sharing his extensive research on Lilian and her life. If I hadn't stumbled across his work on Ancestry.com, this book might never have been. Thanks also to Michael Smith, director of the National Model Aviation Museum, for sharing the museum's research and resources and for always being willing to review my drafts. Special thanks to my husband, Nils Larson, chief pilot at NASA's Armstrong Flight Research Center, and Al Bowers, NASA Armstrong's chief scientist. Your perspectives on flight tests past and present provided valuable context for this story. Finally, thanks to my agent, Lara Perkins, and my editor, Carolyn Yoder, for believing in both me and Lilian, and for helping this story soar from start to finish.

Calkins Creek
An imprint of Astra Books for Young Readers, a division of Astra Publishing House
astrapublishinghouse.com
Printed in China

ISBN: 978-1-62979-938-4 (hc)
ISBN: 978-1-63592-400-8 (eBook)
Library of Congress Control Number: 2019939442

First edition
10 9 8 7 6

Design by Barbara Grzeslo
The text is set in Neutraface Demi.
The illustrations are done in India ink and Chinese brush pen,
walnut ink and bamboo pen, and digital painting.